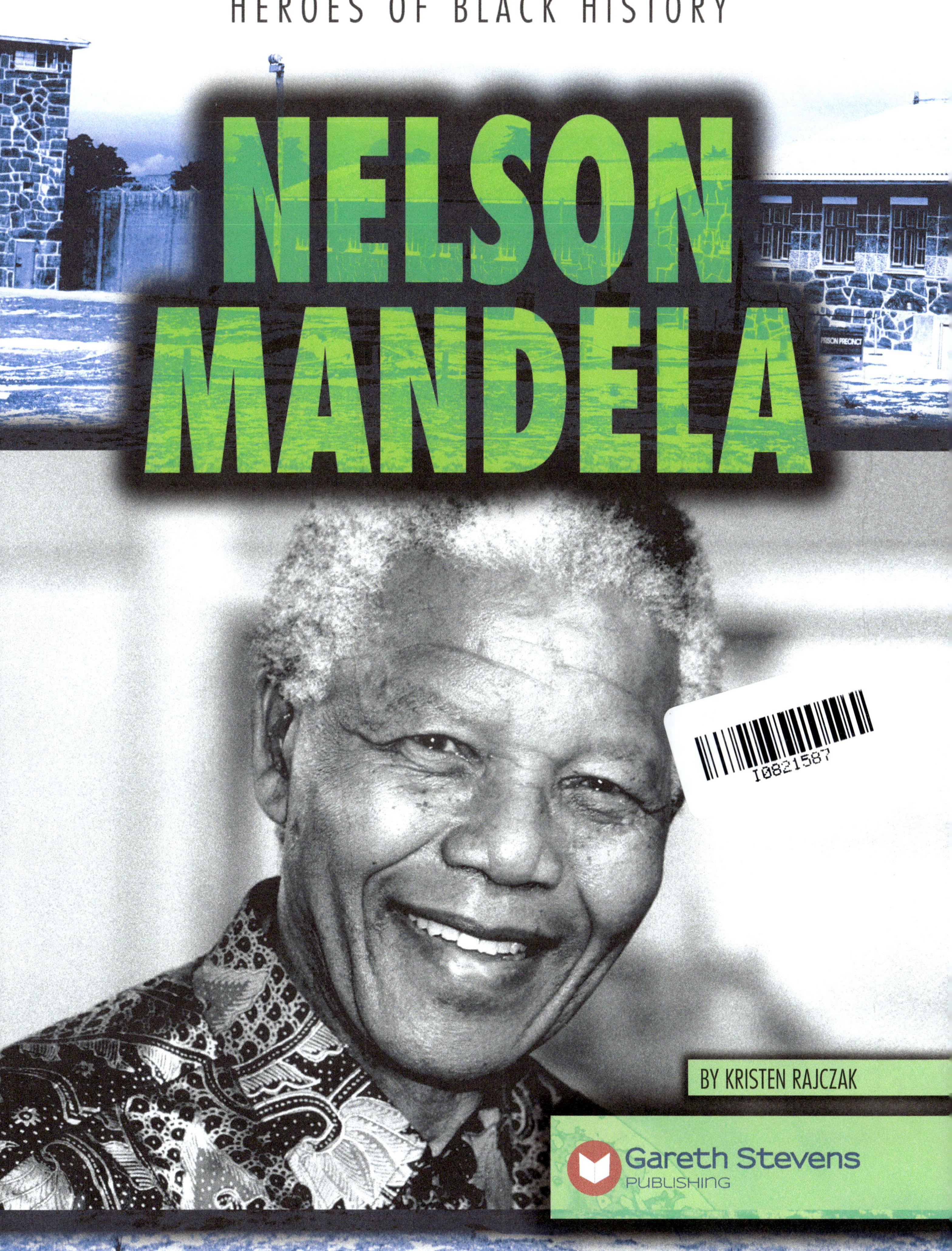
HEROES OF BLACK HISTORY
NELSON MANDELA
BY KRISTEN RAJCZAK
Gareth Stevens
PUBLISHING
I0821587

Please visit our website, www.garethstevens.com. For a free color catalog of all our high-quality books, call toll free 1-800-542-2595 or fax 1-877-542-2596.

Library of Congress Cataloging-in-Publication Data

Rajczak, Kristen
Nelson Mandela / Kristen Rajczak.
pages cm. — (Heroes of Black history)
Includes bibliographical references and index.
ISBN 978-1-4824-2908-4 (pbk.)
ISBN 978-1-4824-2909-1 (6 pack)
ISBN 978-1-4824-2910-7 (library binding)
1. Mandela, Nelson, 1918-2013—Juvenile literature. 2. Presidents—South Africa—Biography—Juvenile literature. 3. Political prisoners—South Africa—Biography—Juvenile literature. 4. Anti-apartheid activists—Juvenile literature. 5. South Africa—Politics and government—1948-1994. 6. South Africa—Politics and government—1994- I. Title. II. Series: Heroes of Black history.
DT1974.R35 2015
968.06'5092—dc23
[B]

2014048105

First Edition

Published in 2016 by
Gareth Stevens Publishing
111 East 14th Street, Suite 349
New York, NY 10003

Designer: Katelyn E. Reynolds
Editor: Therese Shea

Photo credits: Cover, p. 1 Thomas Imo/Photothek/Getty Images; cover, pp. 1–32 (background image) Mark Hannaford/AWL Images/Getty Images; p. 5 Dario Mitidieri/Photonica World/Getty Images; p. 6 Indech/Wikipedia.org; p. 7 Fountain Posters/Wikipedia.org; p. 8 AFP/Getty Images; p. 9 API/Gamma-Rapho via Getty Images; pp. 11, 12, 14 Keystone-France/Gamma-Keystone/Getty Images; p. 13 OFF/AFP/Getty Images; p. 15 STF/AFP/Getty Images; p. 16 Peter Dunne/Getty Images; p. 17 Popperfoto/Getty Images; p. 18 Peter Hermes Furian/Shutterstock.com; p. 19 Express/Archive Photos/Getty Images; p. 21 Alexander Joe/AFP/Getty Images; pp. 23, 25 Walter Dhladhla/AFP/Getty Images; p. 26 Thomas Coex/AFP/Getty Images; p. 27 Felix Dlangamandla/AFP/Getty Images; p. 28 Mike Copeland/Gallo Images/Getty Images.

Printed in the United States of America

CPSIA compliance information: Batch #CS15GS: For further information contact Gareth Stevens, New York, New York at 1-800-542-2595.

CONTENTS

Words in the glossary appear in **bold** type the first time they are used in the text.

A LASTING LEGACY

On December 5, 2013, Nelson Mandela died in his home in Johannesburg, South Africa. He had been in the world spotlight for more than 50 years as a civil rights leader. Mandela spent more than 25 of those years in prison for crimes related to his protest of apartheid, or the system of racial **segregation** in South Africa. Mandela was key in ending apartheid in the early 1990s.

Upon Mandela's death, leaders around the world spoke of his **legacy**. Former US president Bill Clinton said, "All of us are living in a better world because of the life that Madiba lived."

APARTHEID

"Apartheid" means "apartness" in the South African language of Afrikaans (aa-frih-KAHNS). The National Party first used the term in 1948, though apartheid was practiced before then. When the National Party came to power, it made more apartheid laws. For example, the Population Registration Act of 1950 called for South Africans to register as black, white, or colored (a mix of black and white).

"Madiba" is another name for Nelson Mandela used by those he was close to. Madiba is Mandela's clan name, which is similar to a last name, but it connects families even when other names change.

HUMBLE BEGINNINGS

Rolihlahla (khol-ee-HLAA-hlaa) Mandela was born on July 18, 1918, in a small village called Mvezo. His family had a royal background, and Mandela's father worked for the chief of their people. Mandela's family lived in a grass hut with a dirt floor and slept on mats. He learned to be a shepherd when he was just 5 years old. A few years later, he went to school, the first of his brothers and sisters to do so.

Then, when he was 12 years old, Mandela's father died, and the young man became the **ward** of the chief. He started learning leadership skills from him.

TRIBES AND BANTUSTANS

Beginning in the 1950s, apartheid divided land on which black South Africans lived into Bantustans, or Bantu homelands. Citizens of these homelands could only vote in these places. They couldn't participate in the central South African government. Tribal lines and locations were mostly ignored by the government.

On Rolihlahla Mandela's first day of school, his teacher gave him the name "Nelson" because all students had to have an English name.

Mandela was sent to a **boarding school**. His first day was the first time he'd ever worn shoes and the first time he'd ever shaken hands with a white man. He went on to the University College of Fort Hare, but he didn't finish his degree there. Mandela completed his college studies later. He also went to law school.

In 1944, Mandela joined the African National Congress (ANC), a political party representing black South Africans. He then helped start the ANC Youth League, a group founded to improve the leadership in the ANC.

EXPELLED

Mandela didn't finish at Fort Hare because he was expelled, or thrown out, of school for taking part in a student protest in 1940. Mandela, a student leader at school, and his classmates wanted better quality food. Oliver Tambo, a good friend of his and fellow activist, was also expelled after the protest.

Oliver Tambo

Mandela and Oliver Tambo started the first black law firm in South Africa in 1952.

MAKING WAVES

Around the same time his law firm was opening, Mandela was "banned" by the South African government for the first time. He was traveling around the country speaking out against the pass laws. These laws forced nonwhite South Africans to carry identification called passes or pass books in certain, usually whites-only, areas.

In 1955, Mandela was part of writing the Freedom Charter, which asked the government for a **democracy** not based on race. Mandela and more than 100 others were arrested and charged with treason for this. By the time he was released, Mandela and the ANC had even more to be angry about.

WHAT IS BANNING?

From about 1948 to 1991, banning was a common practice meant to quiet those who opposed apartheid. Those who were banned weren't allowed to travel and had to leave certain groups they were a part of, such as the ANC. Banned people also might not be allowed to speak publicly or go to gatherings—even funerals.

TREASON TRIAL

The ACCUSED

DECEMBER 1956

Nelson Mandela

This photo shows the many people arrested for supporting the Freedom Charter. While Mandela was on trial for treason, his first marriage ended. Then, in 1958, he married Nomzamo Winifred "Winnie" Madikizela.

SHARPEVILLE MASSACRE

On March 21, 1960, black South Africans marched to the Sharpeville police station in peaceful protest of the pass laws. Their plan was to turn themselves in for not carrying passes. As the day went on, the crowd grew to about 5,000. Police later said someone started pushing and others threw stones. One police officer got scared and opened fire. Then others did. Sixty-nine people were killed in what's now called the Sharpeville **Massacre**.

Mandela, free after the treason trial, no longer saw the apartheid fight as a peaceful one. He became one of the founders of a military group within the ANC—Spear of the Nation.

GOING UNDERGROUND

Mandela left public life in 1961 to plan **sabotage** of the South African government. In 1962, he went to Algeria to learn ways to challenge those in power. At this time, he was known as the "Black Pimpernel." (The Scarlet Pimpernel was a character in a novel who led a secret life doing good for others.)

Mandela (left) with Algerian Army

The ANC was banned after the Sharpeville Massacre. However, Mandela and the ANC continued to work in secret. A crowd gathers here to support the ANC.

THE RIVONIA TRIAL

Mandela was arrested when he returned to South Africa. He was found guilty of **incitement** and of illegally leaving the country. He was sentenced to 5 years in jail. However, while he began this sentence, he was charged with sabotage, too. Police had found illegal guns and military gear in the Johannesburg suburb of Rivonia and connected Mandela and other ANC leaders to it.

Mandela gave a long speech at the trial highlighting the truth of some of the charges against him, but also the injustices at work in South Africa. Still, he was found guilty and sentenced to life in prison in 1964.

"I AM PREPARED TO DIE"

Mandela ended his trial with a speech in which he said: "I have cherished the ideal of a democratic and free society in which all persons live together in harmony and with equal opportunities. It is an ideal which I hope to live for and to achieve. But if needs be, it is an ideal for which I am prepared to die."

Mandela was nearly put to death. That might seem harsh, but the National Party in power in South Africa was very afraid of the anti-apartheid leaders' plans.

IMPRISONMENT

During his sentence, Mandela was forced to do hard work in prison. His life was lonely, and there wasn't much contact with the outside world. At first, Mandela was only allowed to write two letters a year. Later, he could write as many as two a month, but all his letters were **censored**. He was also allowed few visitors.

However, Mandela was imprisoned with men he knew who were also found guilty in the Rivonia trial. After they were released, many said Mandela was a leader inside the prison walls, just as he had been outside.

FAMILY LOSS

Mandela had two sons and four daughters, one of whom died as a baby. He gave up a lot of time with his family, especially his children, by committing himself to the apartheid struggle. In fact, his son Thembi died in 1969, while he was in prison. Mandela wasn't permitted to go to his son's funeral.

pro-Mandela writing being erased from a wall in 1964

Mandela was imprisoned with Walter Sisulu, another powerful ANC leader and anti-apartheid activist.

Being away from the struggle against apartheid must have been very hard for Mandela. He had given up so much for the cause. Mandela had been known for his hot-tempered personality, so time in jail could have made him a very angry man.

Instead, those who knew Mandela well say he learned to control his anger. He was polite to his jailers as much as possible. A friend wrote in the magazine *Time*: "He came to understand that if he was ever to achieve that free and nonracial South Africa of his dreams, he would have to come to terms with his **oppressors**. He would have to forgive them."

THE REST OF THE WORLD

When Mandela was sent to prison, it only increased black South Africans' love and respect for him. They weren't alone. As the years went on, the international community began to speak out more against apartheid. Mandela turned into the face of the fight, and during his imprisonment, he became known worldwide as a champion of civil rights.

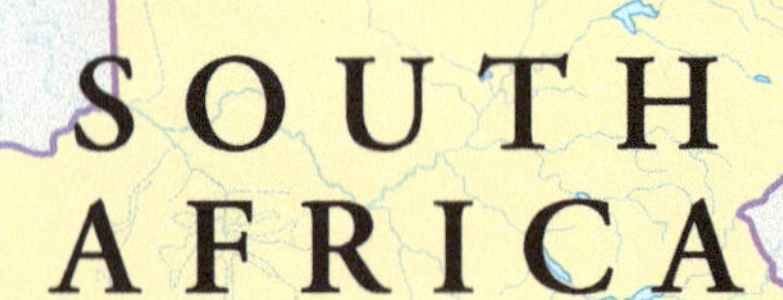

Robben Island Prison was Mandela's home from 1964 to 1982. Here, prisoners break rocks and sew clothes.

FREEDOM ON THE HORIZON

Though sentenced to life in prison, Mandela was offered his freedom several times. But these offers came with conditions, such as accepting the independence of one of the Bantustans and promising to live there. He said no to each offer.

By the 1980s, the political situation in South Africa was truly troubled. When F. W. de Klerk became president in September 1989, he promised change. Mandela first met de Klerk on December 13, 1989, for a secret discussion about South Africa's situation. De Klerk said later he knew he could work with Mandela after that meeting. He arranged for Mandela to be released from prison on February 11, 1990.

CROWDING MANDELA

Mandela was in jail for more than a quarter of a century. In that time, the government wouldn't let anyone see pictures of him. So, the citizens of South Africa didn't know what he might look like. A crowd of 100,000 greeted Mandela as he left Cape Town's City Hall. So many people lined the streets, his car could barely move!

Nelson and Winnie Mandela greet their supporters. He later wrote, "I felt as though the crowd might very well kill us with their love."

ENDING APARTHEID

Mandela was immediately brought back into the African National Congress, where he helped with an agreement to stop the group's fighting. He became president of the party in July 1991.

Mandela and de Klerk worked together to end apartheid. De Klerk led the government in **repealing** the many laws allowing it, and Mandela represented the ANC's interests. They both wanted a peaceful shift to an inclusive democracy.

In 1994, a new **constitution** allowed all South Africans to vote, no matter their race. Mandela voted for the first time in that year's national election, South Africa's first truly democratic election. Mandela was also running in the election.

SHOWING THE WORLD PEACE

Mandela and de Klerk jointly won the Nobel Peace Prize in 1993 for their work peacefully ending apartheid in South Africa. The Nobel committee said in its presentation of the award that Mandela and de Klerk gave hope to South Africa, but were also a "shining example for the world that there are ways out of the vicious circle of violence and bitterness."

Black South Africans had long been the majority in South Africa, leading to a black majority in government after the 1994 elections. However, de Klerk and Mandela made sure the minority races would also be heard.

PRESIDENT MANDELA

Mandela won the first inclusive democratic presidential election in South Africa and was sworn into office on May 10, 1994. As president, he worked to end the injustice of apartheid in effect around the country. Though the laws had been repealed, long-held ways of thinking were hard to change. His Truth and Reconciliation Commission looked into civil rights problems still happening. In addition, improving housing, education, and business growth in black communities was a major concern during Mandela's presidency.

In 1996, Mandela led the country in the adoption of a new constitution. When he left office in 1999, South Africa was still healing, but better off.

WHY NOT RUN AGAIN?

Mandela only served one term as South Africa's first democratically elected president. He likely could have continued to serve as long as he wanted. But Mandela knew that all future presidents would look to his example. He didn't think serving for life—or even several terms—would be good for a new democracy.

Mandela ran for office as a member of the ANC. The three men elected after him were also members of the ANC.

RETIREMENT

Once his presidential term was over, Mandela declared he was retired from public life—but he wasn't really. He remained a loud voice for the rights of the oppressed, particularly those with the disease AIDS and the virus HIV which causes it. Both were spreading rapidly in South Africa.

In 2002, he started a charity called 46664—his prisoner number at Robben Island—to raise awareness and help stop the spread of HIV/AIDS. Mandela had personal reasons for taking on this cause: His son died of an AIDS-related illness in 2005. Mandela's last public appearance was at the 2010 World Cup held in South Africa.

GIVING BACK

Mandela set up several charitable organizations in addition to 46664. In 1995, he began the Nelson Mandela Children's Fund. The Nelson Mandela Foundation was established in 1999 to support international peace and social justice issues. The Mandela Rhodes Foundation offers money for education to promising African students showing strong leadership.

When Mandela died in 2013, his body was taken to Qunu, the village he lived in for most of his childhood. Thousands went to his funeral there.

REMEMBERED

Mandela stepped forward when the black population of South Africa needed a leader who was strong enough to face their oppressors. Once free from prison, he showed that this strength could be used without violence. Mandela devoted his life to shedding light on social justice issues and was able to better the lives of millions of South Africans.

After Mandela's death, F. W. de Klerk spoke of the man with whom he had worked for peace: "I believe that his example will live on and that it will continue to inspire all South Africans to achieve his vision of nonracialism, justice, human dignity, and equality for all."

'ROUND THE WORLD CELEBRATION

When Mandela turned 90 in 2008, several countries celebrated his birthday as Mandela Day, a holiday encouraging people to perform community service all over the world. In 2009, the United Nations chose his July 18 birthday to be an annual holiday to be observed every year, calling it Nelson Mandela International Day.

Many will remember Mandela through the book he wrote about his life, *Long Walk to Freedom.*

TIMELINE OF NELSON MANDELA'S LIFE

1918	Nelson Rolihlahla Mandela is born on July 18.
1930	Mandela's father dies.
1944	Mandela joins the African National Congress.
1948	The National Party comes to power and constructs apartheid policies.
1950	The Population Registration Act passes.
1960	The Sharpeville Massacre of March 21 sparks ANC anger.
1964	Mandela is sentenced to life in prison on June 12.
1990	Mandela is freed by F. W. de Klerk on February 11.
1993	Mandela is awarded the Nobel Peace Prize jointly with de Klerk.
1994	First inclusive democratic election is held in South Africa. Mandela is sworn in as president of South Africa on May 10.
1999	The Nelson Mandela Foundation is established.
2008	Mandela Day is celebrated July 18 for Mandela's 90th birthday.
2009	Nelson Mandela International Day is established.
2013	Mandela dies on December 5.

GLOSSARY

boarding school: a school where students live

censor: to look over and remove anything thought harmful

constitution: the basic laws by which a country or state is governed

democracy: the free and equal right of every person to participate in a government

incitement: the act of causing people to behave in a violent way

legacy: what someone leaves behind, including inspiration from words and actions

massacre: the killing of a large number of people, especially when they cannot defend themselves

oppressor: one who acts harshly or cruelly to keep others from gaining power

repeal: to do away with

sabotage: an act against a government meant to harm it

segregation: the forced separation of races or classes

ward: someone, usually a child, under the protection of another

FOR MORE INFORMATION

BOOKS

Coster, Patience. *The Struggle Against Apartheid*. Mankato, MN: Franklin Watts, 2010.

Doeden, Matt. *Nelson Mandela: World Leader for Human Rights*. Minneapolis, MN: Lerner Publications, 2015.

Gormley, Beatrice. *Nelson Mandela: South African Revolutionary*. New York, NY: Aladdin, 2014.

WEBSITES

African National Congress
www.anc.org.za
Learn more about Nelson Mandela's political party, browse a large number of his speeches, and read about South Africa today.

Apartheid Museum
www.apartheidmuseum.org/content/home
This South African museum's website provides information about the history of apartheid and many interesting exhibits on the subject.

Publisher's note to educators and parents: Our editors have carefully reviewed these websites to ensure that they are suitable for students. Many websites change frequently, however, and we cannot guarantee that a site's future contents will continue to meet our high standards of quality and educational value. Be advised that students should be closely supervised whenever they access the Internet.

INDEX